Super Gross

Night Creatures!

by Maria Le
illustrated by Alison Hawkins

Ready-to-Read

SIMON SPOTLIGHT
An imprint of Simon & Schuster Children's Publishing Division
New York London Toronto Sydney New Delhi
1230 Avenue of the Americas, New York, New York 10020
This Simon Spotlight edition August 2023
Text copyright © 2023 by Simon & Schuster, Inc.
Illustrations copyright © 2023 by Alison Hawkins • Stock photos by iStock
SIMON SPOTLIGHT, READY-TO-READ, and colophon are registered trademarks of Simon & Schuster, Inc.
For information about special discounts for bulk purchases, please contact Simon & Schuster Special Sales at 1-866-506-1949 or
business@simonandschuster.com.
Manufactured in the United States of America 0723 LAK
2 4 6 8 10 9 7 5 3 1
This book has been cataloged by the Library of Congress.
ISBN 978-1-6659-4094-8 (pbk)
ISBN 978-1-6659-4095-5 (hc)
ISBN 978-1-6659-4096-2 (ebook)

Glossary

arachnid: a member of the group of animals that includes spiders, scorpions, ticks, and mites

bioluminescence: the emission of light from living organisms

nocturnal: active at night

predators: living things that kill and eat other living things

opossum: a mammal that lives in the Americas, is a skilled climber, typically has a white face and grayish body, and the female has a fur-lined pouch where the offspring develop after birth

venomous: producing venom in a specialized gland and capable of inflicting injury or death

Note to readers: Some of these words may have more than one definition. The definitions above match how these words are used in this book.

Contents

Chapter 1:
Night Flight

Hello! I'm Dr. Ick,
and like my name suggests,
I love all things icky under the sun.
(And under the moon, too!)
Today we'll discover some creepy
and gross creatures that lurk
in the night.

Most animals are active
during the day, but **nocturnal**
(say: nawk-TUR-nul)
creatures are busy at night.

When the sun sets, these animals
come out to hunt for food.
Some slither on the ground
while others take to the skies.
Let's look up and see!

I'd rather
not.

Introducing the . . . vampire bat!
Vampire bats have webbed wings
that help them fly while they search
for their next meal.

They use their sharp teeth to bite other animals, and then use their tongues to lick up the blood.

But don't worry. Vampire bats' bites are tiny and painless. Their prey don't even wake up when bitten!

Another creature that uses the darkness of night to hunt for food is the barn owl. These ghostly **predators** (say: PREH-duh-terz) swallow their prey whole!

That's disgusting!

But not all nighttime fliers are spooky or icky. Some are small and cute! Like the flying squirrel.

These creatures don't *really* fly. They use the membrane—or thin layer of skin—between their limbs to glide from one point to another.

A lot of nocturnal creatures can be hard to spot in the dark. But the firefly is one of the easiest to find. It has a special organ that produces light. This light production is called **bioluminescence** (say: bie-oh-loo-muh-NEH-sunts).

Fireflies flash these lights to communicate with one another.

That's not too icky.

Chapter 2:
Late-Night Bites

We've seen nocturnal animals
in the sky, but there are plenty
more to discover on the ground.

Some can be quite deadly, like the deathstalker scorpion. This **arachnid** (say: uh-RACK-nid) has a powerful venom that can cause paralysis—the loss of sensation or movement in a part of the body. They use their stinger and venom to hunt their prey.

Some night creatures sting,
while others bite.
The Tasmanian devil may have
the biggest bite of them all.

Their bites are strong
enough to crush bones!

Many night creatures have to be fast to hunt for food.
But the pygmy (say: PIG-mee) slow loris likes to take its time.

It might be slow and small,
but it still packs a big bite—
a **venomous** (say: VEH-nuh-muss)
one at that! This creature licks
the venom on its arms and
mixes it with its saliva for a
painful and dangerous bite!

Ew!

Chapter 3: Nightmarish Creatures

There are many types of yucky creatures that creep in the night, but some of them are stranger than others.

There are creatures with
weird combinations of
body parts from other animals.
Others are scaly like dinosaurs.
Some even play dead!

Do you know what creature has
a bill like a duck, a tail like a beaver,
venom like a snake, and lays eggs
like a bird?

It's a platypus! Platypuses' unique anatomy—or parts of the body—makes them excellent swimmers!

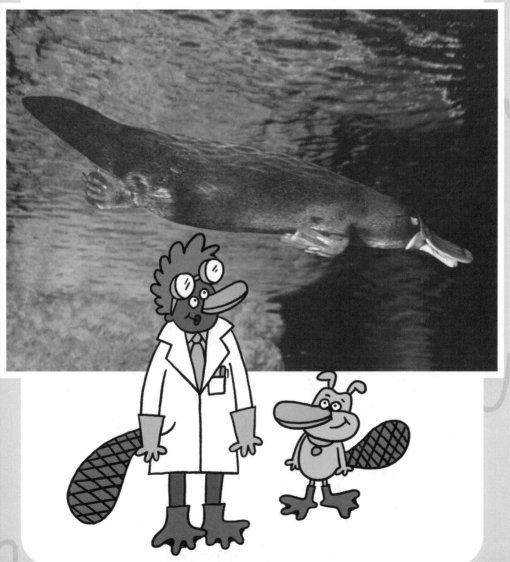

This next night creature
uses its strange anatomy to
protect itself from predators.

Isn't that a
pine cone?

It's a pangolin (say: PANG-guh-luhn)!
These toothless mammals have scales,
but they aren't reptiles. Their scales
are made of the same material as
our fingernails! When threatened,
the pangolin curls up into a ball and
protects itself with its scaly armor.

While some creatures use their anatomy for protection against predators, others use strange behaviors to avoid threats.

The **opossum** (say: uh-PAH-sum)
knows a neat trick: playing dead!
When a predator is near,
the opossum curls up
and pretends to be dead.
It can play dead for hours!

Are you sure it's
pretending?

Don't worry. If left alone,
it will go back to foraging
(say: FOR-ih-jing),
or searching, for food.

Night creatures are fascinating, aren't they, Sam?

I think they're gross!

They can be hard to observe
because they're active at night.
But they still play an important role
in nature. Let's keep our
planet safe for these
creatures of the night!

31

Flying-Squirrel Glider

Nocturnal animals can be hard to spot sometimes, but here's a night creature you can make and keep in your house! In this activity you'll learn how to make a flying squirrel!

You will need:

- a grown-up to help you
- paper
- crayons, markers, or colored pencils

Directions:

1. Fold a paper airplane, or have an adult help you: Fold a piece of paper in half lengthwise. Unfold the paper and fold the top two corners to the centerline. Fold the paper in half again. Fold the short edges to meet the long edges.
2. On the airplane's wings, draw and color a flying squirrel.
3. Let your flying squirrel glide!